PEARISBURG PUBLIC LIBRARY

7 95

DISCARD

D1404913

PLEASE WASH
YOUR HANDS
BEFORE YOU READ ME
AND KEEP ME CLEAN

WORD BIRD'S
SUMMER WORDS

by Jane Belk Moncure
illustrated by Linda Hohag

THE CHILD'S WORLD

ELGIN, ILLINOIS 60120

J E
Mo

Distributed by Childrens Press, 1224 West Van Buren Street, Chicago, Illinois 60607.

Library of Congress Cataloging in Publication Data

Moncure, Jane Belk.
    Word Bird's summer words.

    (Word house words for early birds)
    Summary: Word Bird puts words about summer in his word house—swimming pool, seashells, boat, fireworks, lemonade, parade, and others.
    1. Vocabulary—Juvenile literature.   2. Summer—Juvenile literature.   [1. Vocabulary.   2. Summer]
I. Hohag, Linda, ill.   II. Title.   III. Series: Moncure, Jane Belk.   Word house words for early birds.
PE1449.M533   1985   428.1   85-5930
ISBN 0-89565-311-7

© 1985 The Child's World, Inc.
All rights reserved. Printed in U.S.A.

1 2 3 4 5 6 7 8 9 10 11 12 R 91 90 89 88 87 86 85

1533

WORD BIRD'S
SUMMER WORDS

57497 0 c…… 17

Word Bird made a ...

word house.

"I will put summer words
in my house," he said.

He put in these words –

park

swimming pool

bathing suit

splash

beach ball

seashells

shovel and pail

sand castle

boat

fish

flowers

butterfly

lawn mower

lemonade

picnic

watermelon

ice cream

the Fourth of July

parade

flags

fireworks

fireflies

tent

sleeping bag

Can you read these summer word

park

pail

swimming pool

sand castle

bathing suit

boat

splash

beach ball

fish

seashells

flowers

shovel

butterfly

ith ? **WORD BIRD**

the Fourth of July

lawn mower

parade

lemonade

flags

picnic

fireworks

watermelon

fireflies

ice cream

tent

sleeping bag

PEARISBURG PUBLIC LIBRARY

You can make a summer word house. You can put Word Bird's words in your house and read them too.

PEARISBURG PUBLIC LIBRARY